SAN ANTONIO MISSIONS

by
Luis Torres

photography by
George H. H. Huey

SOUTHWEST PARKS AND MONUMENTS ASSOCIATION
TUCSON, ARIZONA

INTRODUCTION

THREE CENTURIES AGO, Spain's territorial claims to lands north and west of the Gulf of Mexico were tenuous. The fertile plains of what is now southern Texas lay on the outer frontier of a far-flung colonial empire, and here Spanish civilization had yet to gain a foothold. The headwaters of the San Antonio River were a two-week hard ride beyond the northernmost settlements of New Spain early in 1718, when Franciscan fathers arrived to establish the first of an eventual five missions.

Representing both church and state, these missions were charged with converting the free-roaming, hunting-and-gathering natives into devoutly Catholic, Spanish-speaking peasant farmers loyal to the one true God and the Spanish Crown. More than mere churches in the wilderness, the San Antonio missions served as pioneer vocational education centers, great economic enterprises involved in both agricultural and livestock production, and active participants in the developing trade of the region.

The missions formed the foundation for what is today the thriving, multi-cultural metropolis of San Antonio. They also provide a vital link to the living legacy of Spain and Mexico in the United States, and thus are truly national treasures.

Mission San Antonio, "The Alamo," has been converted into a shrine to Texas state patriotism. The other four are protected as units of San Antonio Missions National Historical Park, and what has been preserved is both venerable and vestigial.

Ruins of the uncompleted church at Mission San Juan.

OPPOSITE — Church and convento of Mission San José.

The compound wall of Mission San José.

At Mission San José, one can see how a mission complex appeared and imagine what life at a mission must have been like, yet much of what exists is reconstructed. Not much remains of the Mission Concepción complex beyond the handsome church and a handful of rooms from the old *convento*, but these are almost entirely original.

The more remote remnants of missions San Juan and Espada are preserved in largely agrarian settings. Not far from Espada, a dam and aqueduct still divert water from the San Antonio River. Near San Juan, original *labores*, or farm fields, and an *acequia*, or irrigation ditch, are part of the Mission San Juan Spanish Colonial Demonstration Farm.

A visit to the San Antonio missions inevitably stimulates more questions. One can get a sense of the devotion, effort, and artistry involved in their construction, but the important roles the missions played in the history of the region are less apparent. Much of their story remains to be discovered by visitors.

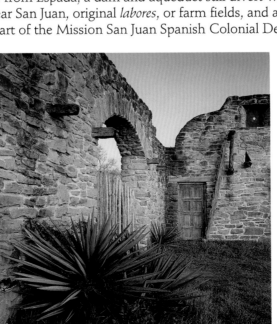

VICEROYALTY IN NEW SPAIN. Following Christopher Columbus' epochal first voyage at the end of the fifteenth century, Spain and the other European powers joined in a race to find and claim further "new" lands, explore them, and finally control, settle, and exploit them. Having just reconquered its national territory by defeating the Moors at Granada in 1492, the Spanish Crown and the entire Spanish nation were primed to engage in adventure and enterprise. The recently expanded geographic horizons were made to order for this purpose.

But Spain was interested in more than simply defeating the great native civilizations of this new world, taking their riches, and returning home. Spain set out to transplant its language, culture, religion, legal system, and form of government; to create, in other words, a *Spanish America*. Following the *conquistadores* came the administrators, the exploiters, the colonizers, and the missionaries. For the missionaries, the biggest attraction of the Americas was the thousands of heathen natives to be converted to Christianity.

Earliest-known image of American Indians, ca. 1505.

From the mid-sixteenth century through the end of the seventeenth century Spain consolidated its power and established a Spanish presence by conquering the native inhabitants. The conquest of highly sophisticated, complex, and widespread civilizations, such as the Aztecs and the Incas, was especially bloody. When dealing with smaller and less complex communities, with widely scattered peoples such as the natives of today's Texas, or with highly mobile peoples such as the Apaches and Comanches, conquest and pacification took different forms.

Once the power of the native empires was broken, Spanish colonists could safely arrive in greater numbers. The great cities of Spanish America began taking shape as civilian administrators representing the Crown arrived and assumed their duties. In the countryside, soldiers who had been involved in the conquest were granted access to free and forced Indian labor as part of the pacification process. At the same time, Indians were gathered into segregated villages, where they could be Christianized, incorporated into the Spanish administrative system, and controlled.

Under a system of *repartimientos*, Indians were divided among the new land owners and often were reduced to virtual slavery. Eventually reforms were undertaken and the *encomienda* system was introduced, under which land and the Indians upon it were "put in trust" in the hands of Spaniards, who were supposed to give their charges instruction in the Christian religion. Indians in the encomienda were theoretically granted legal rights similar to those of feudal peasants in Spain, whose obligations to the feudal lord were, to some extent, balanced by recognized rights. Still, Indian labor was free to the Spanish and enforced by the Crown. Abuses continued until the encomienda system was abolished.

The area that today encompasses Mexico, California, and the American Southwest became part of the Viceroyalty of New Spain, whose seat of government was in Mexico City. While the pacification and colonization of New Spain progressed, other

European powers sought to secure a part of the Americas. By the early seventeenth century, England and France were exploring north of the territory claimed by Spain. The English established colonies along the northeastern coast of North America. The French probed the Mississippi River in 1681 and 1682, and sought to control the area that would eventually be named Louisiana.

Rumors of these foreign incursions along the edges of its territory forced Spain to devote more resources to the exploration and colonization of the northeasterly border areas of New Spain. The missions of Texas were a major part of Spain's efforts to bolster its claim to the region.

ADVANCE AND RETREAT IN THE BORDERLANDS. As Spanish control of the heart of New Spain became more firmly established, what is now the Mexican state of Chihuahua was colonized and missions were established among the Pueblo Indians of present-day New Mexico. Eventually, royal authorities began to turn their attention to the northeast, particularly to Nuevo León and Coahuila, where silver had been discovered. The Spanish gradually overcame resistance from the unpacified Indians of the area, and by 1674 four missions had been established for the Indians of Coahuila.

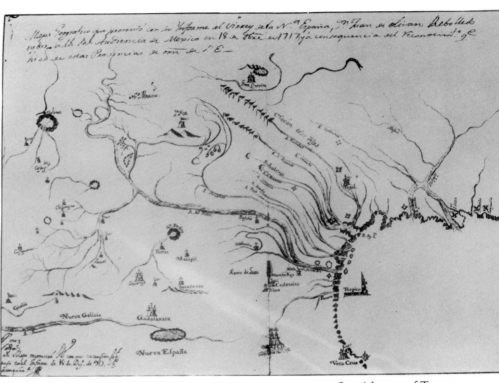

Spanish map of Texas in 1717, showing the Mission San Francisco de los Tejas and other missions.

News of thrusts by LaSalle, from the French-controlled area around the mouth of the Mississippi south along the Gulf Coast, were deemed an immediate threat to New Spain's northern territories. The capture of one of LaSalle's ships raised the alarm. Land and sea searches ordered by the Viceroy of New Spain went on for five years before the French fort was finally discovered in 1689 near Matagorda Bay. Only its remains were found, for it had been destroyed by internal dissension and Indian attacks. These expeditions north of the Rio Grande, together with pressure from missionaries anxious to begin work there, encouraged the authorities to seek colonial control of the area.

Alonso de León, governor of Coahuila, inaugurated the Spanish colonization of Texas with an expedition in 1690. Accompanied by Fr. Damián Massanet from the Missionary College of the Holy Cross of Querétaro, who kept a chronicle of the expedition, de León explored northeast Texas and established Mission San Francisco de los Tejas (for the Tejas Indians), near San Pedro Creek in today's Houston County.

The first governor of the province of Texas and adjacent regions, Domingo Terán de los Ríos, led another expedition in 1691. Fr. Massanet accompanied this expedition, as well. Their instructions were to establish missions among the Tejas Indians, and to keep records of the geography, nature, and native inhabitants of the territory. On 13 June 1691 Terán and Fr. Massanet became the first Europeans to encounter the San Antonio River, which they named in honor of San Antonio de Padua, whose feast day falls on that date.

Fr. Massanet and the missionaries who accompanied him arrived at Mission San Francisco de los Tejas on 2 August. Mission San Francisco lasted only three years, since the Tejas evinced little interest in mission life and the fathers were not able to survive on their own. That first missionary effort, however, confirmed the Franciscan's determination to bring their faith to the Indians of the frontier territories. Subsequent missionary involvement coincided with a reorganization of Franciscan missionary enterprises throughout the Spanish dominions. Apostolic colleges were created specifically to train new missionaries and help direct their work.

In 1716 Captain Domingo Ramón was sent to East Texas with several missionaries, among them Fr. Isidro Félix de Espinosa, who had been in the area with a previous

FRANCISCAN FRIARS The missionaries who operated the Texas missions were Franciscans, members of the First Order of Friars Minor, a mendicant or begging order founded by St. Francis of Assisi in the Middle Ages and pledged to personal poverty and obedience. The Franciscans were not monks, since they were not attached to monastic institutions. Throughout the order's history Franciscans have distinguished themselves for their work among the poor and for their involvement in missionary work worldwide.

Franciscans first came to the Americas with the *conquistadores*. Their brethren and members of other orders arrived in larger numbers soon after the conquest. By 1700 there were 927 Franciscan friaries in the Spanish colonies with a total of 10,802 friars. At the end of the seventeenth and beginning of the eighteenth centuries, apostolic colleges were organized within the order to regulate missionary work throughout Spain's colonial domains. The colleges provided stability and security to the missions, prepared new missionaries, and served as retreats to which individual missionaries could return for physical and spiritual renewal.

In the Americas, the apostolic colleges' mission was to work among the Indian populations. Three were active in New Spain by the mid-eighteenth century, and two of these were involved in the Texas missions. The *Colegio de la Santa Cruz de Querétaro* (College of the Holy Cross of Querétaro) was established in 1683. Fr. Massanet, chronicler of some early expeditions into Texas, was one of the founders. The *Colegio de Nuestra Señora de Guadalupe de Zacatecas* (College of Our Lady of Guadalupe of Zacatecas), was founded in 1706 by Fr. Antonio Margil de Jesús.

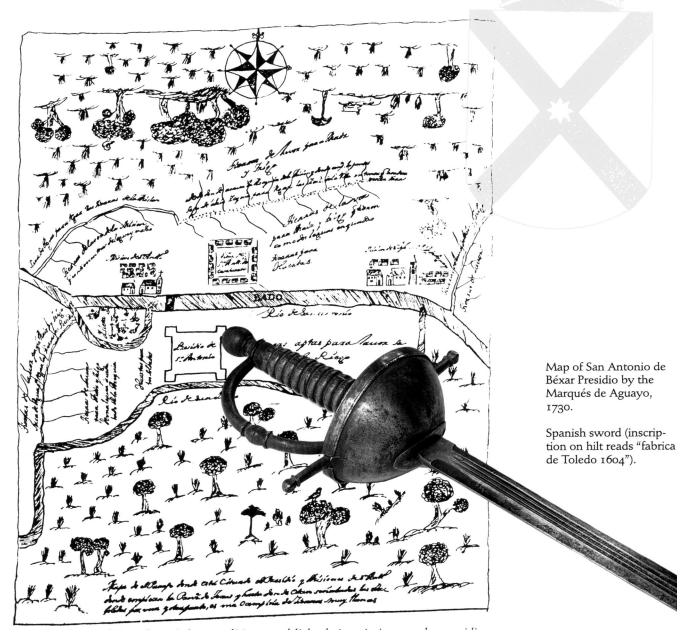

Map of San Antonio de Béxar Presidio by the Marqués de Aguayo, 1730.

Spanish sword (inscription on hilt reads "fabrica de Toledo 1604").

entrada, or expedition. Ramón's expedition established six missions and a *presidio*, or military detachment. The Franciscans from the College of Querétaro re-established Mission San Francisco de los Tejas beyond the Neches River, and added Mission Nuestra Señora de la Purísima Concepción de los Hasinai beyond the Angelina River, and Mission San José de los Nazonis to the northeast of Mission Concepción. Franciscans from the College of Our Lady of Guadalupe of Zacatecas established Mission Nuestra Señora de Guadalupe de los Nacogdoches near present-day Nacogdoches, Mission Nuestra Señora de los Dolores de los Ais in what is today San Augustine County, and Mission San Miguel de los Linares de los Adaes near what is today Robeline, Louisiana.

By the end of 1716 Spain and France were at war, and hostilities spilled over to the Americas. As soon as these missions in East Texas were established, it became obvious that the distances between the governmental centers of New Spain and this exposed flank were too great. The trip from Mexico City, the capital of New Spain, to Nacogdoches took three months. Inclement weather, unfordable rivers, or Indian attacks could cause delays of several days or weeks.

A halfway station and support point was necessary to maintain a strong Spanish presence in East Texas. The San Antonio River was the logical choice. In May 1718, the governor of the province of Texas, Don Martín de Alarcón, and Fr. Antonio de San Buenaventura y Olivares of the College of Queré-taro, arrived to establish Mission San Antonio de Valero and a nearby military garrison and village, the Presidio y Villa de Béxar.

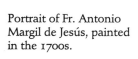

In 1719 the French forced the Spanish missionaries to aban-don their foundations in East Texas and take refuge on the San Antonio River. Once there, one of the refugees, Fr. Antonio Margil de Jesús, who had been in charge of the three East Texas missions of the College of Zacatecas, sought and received authorization from the Marqués de Aguayo, recently appointed governor of Coahuila and Texas, to establish a second mission on the San Antonio River. Mission San José y San Miguel de Aguayo was founded in 1720.

Spanish forces under Aguayo re-established control over East Texas in 1721, and the missionaries were allowed to go back and resume their work at the East Texas missions. By the end of Aguayo's tenure as governor of Coahuila and Texas, the number of missions in the area had expanded to ten and the number of presidios to four. In 1731 Aguayo brought fifty-five immigrants from the Canary Islands to establish a civilian settle-ment, San Fernando de Béxar, on the banks of the San Antonio River, further strengthening the Spanish colonial presence in the area. The city of San Antonio ultimately developed from the presidio and villa of San Antonio de Béxar, the civilian settlement of San Fernando de Béxar, and the missions.

Portrait of Fr. Antonio Margil de Jesús, painted in the 1700s.

HUNTING AND GATHERING NATIVES.

Knowledge of the original inhabitants of the area is slight. They had ceased to exist as a distinct culture by the early nineteenth century. Even the name most commonly given to them by modern scholars—Coahuil-tecans—is based on assumptions that don't bear closer scrutiny. It is not known if they were members of a cultural-linguistic family and spoke dialects of one root language.

The Spanish, who had direct contact with them, left only superficial, fragmentary, and strongly culturally-biased accounts of those contacts, as did most Europeans when they initially came in contact with Native Americans. The Indians were regarded as a problem to be resolved. Their culture and way of life was considered unspeakably poor

"A FINE COUNTRY" What was this northeast corner of New Spain like when the Spanish arrived? One of the earliest available descriptions was recorded by Gen. Domingo Terán de los Ríos in 1691:

> We marched five leagues (thirteen miles) over a fine country with broad plains—the most beautiful in New Spain. We camped on the banks of an *arroyo*, adorned by a great number of trees, cedars, willows, cypresses, osiers, oaks, and many other kinds. . . . This I called San Antonio de Padua because we had reached it on his day.

Fr. Damián Massanet also wrote in his June 1691 diary:

> Low hills [were] covered with oaks and mesquites. The country is very beautiful. . . . Before reaching the [San Antonio] river there are other small hills with large oaks. The river is bordered with many trees, cottonwoods, oaks, cedars, mulberries, and many vines. There are a great many fish and upon the highlands a great number of wild chickens. On this day, there were so many buffalo that the horses stampeded and forty head ran away. . . .

In 1716 Capt. Domingo Ramón noted in his diary that the waters of the San Antonio River only came up to their stirrups. He also mentioned hemp growing nine feet tall and flax two feet high, and adds: "Fish was caught in abundance for everyone, and nets were used in the river with facility." Other accounts talk of eel, catfish, "sardines," and a great variety of other fish, and described alligators populating the banks of rivers and other water courses. Deer, mountain lions or pumas, wolves, coyotes, bears, rabbits and jackrabbits, squirrels, wildcats, and javelinas were reported in abundance.

Capt. Pagés in 1767 said: "The object of my greatest surprise in this part of the world is the immense swarms of cranes which frequent the borders of the rivers."

Fr. Agustín de Morfi made the following notes in 1778:

> There are squirrels of different species, the most beautiful are very light gold with a red belly. . . . Never in my life have I seen such a multitude of ducks, geese, and cranes as those I admired in these fields where the grain had just been harvested; I do not exaggerate when I say that they covered the entire prairie.

Before the arrival of the Spanish, the natives generally lived in small family groups, but gatherings of five hundred to three or four thousand Indians were reported as early as 1709.

Their impact upon the land was less profound than that of the Europeans, who established permanent settlements, began tilling the soil, rechanneled rivers to water crops, and introduced cattle, horses, sheep, and goats. After 1750, these new animals existed in large ranch herds, as well as in substantial numbers gone wild or acquired by Indians. They replaced the vast herds of buffalo and deer that had been hunted or frightened away.

The San Antonio River and lush riparian habitat.

and primitive, not worthy of a second thought. The objective was to convert and "civilize" the native population along the Spanish model as quickly as possible.

Names of groups or bands appear in documents, as do occasional words or phrases in their language or languages, but there is no consistency. Some terms appear to be what the Indians called themselves; other terms may be the Spanish names for particular bands or groups. Variations in the rendition of names in contemporary accounts make it difficult to determine to which group or groups particular documents refer. Period documents provide a considerable catalog of names of bands or groups, but say relatively little about the people. About 150 different groups are associated with the San Antonio River missions alone, with some groups represented at the missions by only one individual.

The Franciscans did some pioneer work in other parts of the world, learning the language and understanding the culture of peoples among whom they did missionary work. In fact, Spanish law regulating missions originally required the missionaries to speak the local language. But in the province of Texas, they may have been overwhelmed by the extent of the area's cultural and linguistic diversity, and repelled by what they saw as the primitiveness of the people. Because the Indians spoke so many different languages, Spanish became the *lingua franca* at the San Antonio missions, both between Indian and missionary and among Indians from different groups.

A language scholars today identify as "Coahuilteco" was spoken in various forms and dialects by a large number of the area's inhabitants. It is also the best documented language, since two missionaries used it in manuals for the administration of church rituals. Other languages or language families may have been spoken in the area, but the record is fragmentary and speculative.

The Coahuiltecans lived in an area that extends from approximately present-day El Paso to the coastal plain, then south across the Rio Grande into the region that now includes the Mexican states of Tamaulipas, Nuevo León, and Coahuila. Their neighbors were the Tejas, who inhabited what is today northeastern Texas, and a number of groups from the Tonkawan linguistic family, located between the Tejas and the Coahuiltecans.

Descriptions of the Coahuiltecans are generally negative. Father Vicente Santa María, a Franciscan traveling with an expedition into Tamaulipas in 1744, was scandalized by the general nudity of these Indians, and by what he described as their "drunkenness and thievery as daily occupations, and fraud and treachery as general and supreme principles." Nonetheless, he had to admit that

> . . . in these barbarians one saw bodies so well formed, so robust, agile, and freed [of blemishes] that among them the number of defects is much reduced: chronic infirmities are extraordinary, and, if, by chance, they do suffer some [infirmity] it will be of short duration. Through their robustness and agility, 50 or 100 leagues [130–260 miles] are like 10 or 20 [26–52 miles] for any others. They find little difference between level ground and the craggiest marches, and to this the better part of them add a height which is common to them and which among us would be singular.

Human remains discovered in 1969 at Mission San Juan, one of the missions in San Antonio Missions National Historical Park, showed "a mean average height of five

Artist's conception of Coahuiltecan Indian carrying a burden.

feet, seven inches for men and five feet, four inches for women. The people were generally narrow faced with high vaulted heads, and noses of medium width."

Tattooing and body painting were widely practiced. Clothing varied: in some groups men wore a deerskin loincloth, while the women wore a knee-length dress made of two deerskins. In the San Antonio area, some groups dressed in untanned animal hides. Some wore shoulder robes or mantles, while others had robes of woven strips of rabbit fur for protection against cold weather. Shell, stone, feathers, bone, and wood were used to make ear, nose, or lip ornaments, as well as necklaces and bracelets.

The Coahuiltecans were hunters and gatherers, moving with the seasons as food availability dictated, using their knowledge of the surroundings to locate food sources. They lived in small bands of a few family groups. Their shelters were rudimentary: bell-shaped *jacales* made of reeds or grass over a frame of bent stalks or canes, set up without any formal arrangement. Their possessions were few. They carried everything they owned or needed as they moved from one location to the next.

Their diet consisted of seasonal fruit, berries, nuts, seeds, and roots, supplemented by a variety of animals, birds, and fish. They hunted with bows and arrows, spears, and "rabbit clubs," and fished with bows and arrows or nets. Flint knives and scrapers were used for a variety of purposes. A report of Fr. Ignacio Antonio Ciprián, of the College of Zacatecas, described how these people secured their food:

> As to how best to describe how they spend their time, they use it in preparing storage places and filling them with the fruit of their harvest and with what the forest supplies in such abundance. They make cakes of persimmons, which they dry and preserve. They cook chestnuts, and having removed the shell, they dry them under the sun and keep them in sacks. They fill their small granaries with acorns and pecans and are so eager in gathering them that in a few days after the fruit of the tree falls to the ground, it is picked up. Not one nut is left on the ground, even though the forest is thick and more than three fourths of the trees are walnut and oak. Other fruit which they cannot keep, such as blackberries, dewberries, strawberries, Chinese pomegranates, plums, and the fruit of the texocote or bushy dew-tree serve as food to appease their appetites in their various seasons.

The Coahuiltecans used chert scrapers and flint knives for a variety of purposes.

Spanish secular reporters and the missionaries dismissed Coahuiltecan ceremonialism and world view as "superstition." The Coahuiltecans had wise men, shamans, or medicine men, and recurring social-religious observances that the Spaniards called *mitotes*. These marked the changing seasons and involved gatherings of many groups, fasting, singing, dancing, the exchange of gifts, and the use of various hallucinogens.

By the time the San Antonio missions were established, the Indians of the area were hard pressed. The northward thrust of Spanish colonization had pushed them out of the southernmost ranges of their territory, and the inexorable advance into Texas brought European intruders into the remainder of it. Simultaneously, they were pressured by the Apache peoples, who were being displaced from territories to the north. By the end of the seventeenth century, Apaches had acquired horses from the Spanish and had become a very effective mobile threat to the Coahuiltecans and, eventually, the Spanish themselves. Displaced and demoralized both by Apaches and the Spanish, the Coahuiltecans were compelled to accept Christianity and join the missions that were being established for them.

MISSIONS FOR CROSS AND CROWN. In a sense, the mission became the successor to the encomienda system as a means of controlling the natives of the conquered territories and incorporating them into the Spanish colonial administrative system. Instead of being placed in the hands of individual Spaniards, Indians were now placed in the hands of the church, whose representatives were charged with safeguarding the Indians' interests. Instead of being coerced into the system, Indians were now supposed to enter it voluntarily.

Since Spain lacked the manpower to colonize the territories it claimed, missions served to transform the native population into Spanish settlers who would serve as a buffer against enemy intrusion. These "Spanish settlements" helped legitimize Spain's claim to new territory. The Indians were subjected to a *reducción* (reduction), whereby they were rounded-up and brought to live in formally established mission compounds. There, they were converted to Christianity, taught Spanish and instructed in the rudiments of Spanish civilization, and taught the agricultural methods and crafts that were useful in the context of a Spanish peasant community.

A successful mission, usually with a small garrison at a nearby presidio for support and protection, established a clear Spanish presence in the border areas, and supported eventual colonization. Theoretically, once Spanish settlements were established and Indians had successfully completed their mission experience, they were to be incorporated into Spanish colonial society with the same rights and obligations as Europeans. This process was expected to take about ten years, at which time the missions were to be secularized, a process that was supposed to take several predetermined stages.

After the initial period of mission activity, a second stage called *doctrina*, or partial secularization, was reached. At this point, the missionaries turned over the management of the community to a government made up of Indian converts. The missionary remained on the scene supervising the continued religious instruction of the community and functioning, in effect, as a parish priest.

The final stage, *curato*, required the missionary to turn over the mission congregation and its church to the secular clergy as a regular parish under the authority of the local bishop. Since the mission churches were built and furnished at the expense of the Crown, they were thus "returned" to the Crown. Lands and property of the mission were to be divided among the converted Indians, and the mission community became a new *pueblo*, or town.

In the northernmost frontier area, the theory did not work in practice. The missions along the San Antonio River, for example, lasted for several decades rather than just for one. Some critics maintain that, once in operation, the missions acquired a life of their own as institutions and that the missionaries had a vested interest in keeping them in operation. Other scholars believe that the ten-year schedule was unrealistic because, at least for a period, the missions had to deal with a continued influx of unconverted Indians who had to be incorporated into the institution. Documents of the period also show that in some cases the missionaries resisted secularization because they feared—with good reason—that their charges would become easy prey for land grabbers and other exploiters once they were removed from the protection of the mission.

The missions were a curious mixture of religious and civil institutions, a mixture that reflected the relation between the Spanish church and the Spanish state under the *patronato real*. Established at the time of Ferdinand and Isabella by a papal decree of 1508, the patronato real granted the Spanish monarchs the right to collect tithes and approve church appointments, directives, and finances in the New World. The missionaries were thus considered employees of the state. In addition to personal expenses, each Franciscan received a royal allowance for a new habit, books, and other necessary equipment.

Once in New Spain, the missionaries were under the supervision and ultimate authority of the viceroy and his officials, as representatives of the Crown. However, just as priests and members of religious orders were enjoined from meddling in civil matters, the civil authorities were instructed not to interfere in the internal affairs of religious orders and their missions. Within the missionary orders, the missions were grouped into districts headed by a Father President, who was usually also a missionary.

Although administered by the church, each mission received from the royal treasury an *ayuda de costa*, or "start-up" grant to cover the cost of bells, vestments, tools, and other necessities, and individual missionaries were paid annual *sínodos*, which varied depending on difficulty of the mission assignment. Occasional emergency grants came from the state treasury. The state also provided land grants with which the missions, and eventually the converted Indians, could support themselves, and provided military protection, stationed at the nearby presidios and at each of the missions. Expenses for the missions and the presidios were charged to the same account by the royal treasury.

Older missions helped establish new foundations, and often private individuals gave special gifts to help carry on the mission work. Funds from the state and other sources belonged to the mission as an institution. Individual missionaries received an annual salary, which they often spent to supplement their mission's budget or to cover additional needs. The missionary orders in Mexico also supported their brethren on the frontier by soliciting contributions and organizing supply trains that traveled to the missions at least once a year. The missions were never self-sufficient, since they depended on these supply trains for many necessities. They brought food items that were not available on the frontier, clothing for both missionaries and Indians, tools and utensils, church wine and vestments, and other articles.

Mission Indians, once acculturated, were used as scouts or as supplementary forces to protect the missions, presidios, or civilian settlements against Apache and Comanche raiders. Successful missions also played a very important part in the agriculture and commerce of frontier settlements, often helping support the colonial Spanish population by selling surplus agricultural production and employing Spanish craftspeople to do jobs that could not yet be performed by mission Indians.

This seventeenth-century woodcut figure depicts the Virgin Mary as a Spanish nun.

Missions became almost universal in Spain's administrative scheme for its frontier territories, and were a major influence well into the eighteenth century. They were established throughout what is today northern Mexico, as well as California, Florida, New Mexico, Texas, and Arizona. Franciscan, Jesuit, Dominican, and Augustinian friars founded and administered them. When the Jesuits were expelled from the Americas in 1767 by colonial authorities, other orders took their place.

Outposts in the wilderness. Missionary fathers must have been men of exceptional faith, dedication, and courage. Whether born in Spain or in Spanish America, they left the known world behind to minister to people they little understood, with nothing but discomfort, hard work, and deprivation as their immediate reward. Aside from the daily work of running the missions, they had to deal with superiors at the apostolic colleges in Querétaro and Zacatecas, with local military authorities at the presidio, and with local and provincial civil authorities. Most were ill-equipped to cope with serious illness and injuries.

Missions began with very little. Missionaries and Indians alike initially lived in jacales while they cleared farmland, planted crops to feed the community, and constructed irrigation ditches. As late as 1740 Captain Toribio Urrutia, commander of the presidio of San Antonio, described conditions at the missions as primitive. In a letter to the Viceroy, Urrutia reported that some of the mission churches still had thatch roofs, while others had collapsed entirely. "The Indians have no houses nor protection, for as they are new at work, and spend most of the year planting, digging irrigation ditches, and making dams, they can only build little by little."

Missionary fathers operated under primitive conditions in the early days.

The mission's daily routine and ultimate physical configuration evolved from the medieval monastic communities of Europe, particularly those of the Benedictine monks, and were adapted to the needs of the Americas. Gradually, as each mission became more successful, the missionaries built a more permanent, and more grand, church or chapel. There Mass was said, baptisms, weddings, and funerals were held, and at least some religious instruction took place. A *camposanto*, or cemetery, was located next to, or near, the church.

Adjacent to the church, and sometimes connected to it, was a *convento*. This complex of rooms included quarters for the resident missionaries and visitors, office or work rooms, a granary where crops, seeds, and other household supplies were stored, a kitchen, and a refectory or dining room. Quarters for mission soldiers were nearby.

Also in the convento or in nearby space were rooms where Indians learned and worked on various crafts. These might include carding wool, spinning and weaving both wool and cotton, and carpentry and wood carving. There was also a blacksmith shop. In some cases, there were work spaces devoted to masonry, tanning, brick- and tile-making, basketry, and ceramics, and a room for preserving food with salt and chile.

Often in front of the church there was a wide *plaza*, or open space. Some church activities might take place there, including processions, feast day observances, and even church-sanctioned Indian dances, such as that of the *matachines*, with masked dancers accompanied by guitars and violins. (A version of the matachines dance is still performed occasionally at Mission San José; other versions are danced in New Mexico, southern Arizona, and parts of Mexico.) Classes in doctrine, Spanish language, or music; or rudimentary military drill for the men, might also be held in the plaza.

Each Indian family was assigned its own living space. For defense against Indian attacks, the mission's Indian housing formed part of a defensive perimeter wall around the mission, which also included gates and defensive structures. The following report of 1758 attests:

> The mission has 84 flat-roofed homes of stone arranged according to a plan, each home with an *azotea* [a living-working area on the flat roof], and crenelated security walls on the roof, the homes divided up into four quarters. Each home consists of a room and a kitchen, and is equipped with a *metate* [with its corresponding *mano* for grinding corn], a pot, a *comal* [or grill for baking tortillas], a water jar, a place to hang clothes, a chest, a bed, baskets and storage boxes, and a water tank. Each of the quarters has eighteen houses, each arranged in the same way to form enclosed patios in which there are ovens.

Immediately outside the wall were the *huertas*, orchards or small gardens, and beyond them were the *labores*, or larger farm fields where they planted corn, squash, beans, chiles, sugarcane, or cotton. Mission farming required irrigation, and among the first tasks undertaken was the construction of *acequias*, irrigation ditches with sluices and gates to bring water from the San Antonio River to the fields and mission. Some acequia systems were quite complex, and two still operate within the San Antonio Missions National Historical Park.

Beyond the labores—often twenty miles or more—were the mission ranches where cattle, horses, sheep, and goats were raised. Some Indian *vaqueros*, or cowboys, lived at these ranches in stone huts, such as at Rancho de las Cabras, twenty-five miles from Mission Espada. Working these ranches was hazardous, since they presented a relatively easy target for hostile Indians.

Metates and manos were used for grinding corn and acorns.

MISSION SAN ANTONIO DE VALERO. The roots of Mission San Antonio de Valero are usually traced to Mission San Francisco de Solano on the banks of the Rio Grande, maintained for the Jarame Indians by its founder, Fr. Antonio de San Buenaventura Olivares, from the College of Querétaro.

In 1709 Fr. Olivares, now in the last year of his term as head of the College of Querétaro, joined Capt. Pedro de Aguirre and another Franciscan, Fr. Isidro de Espinosa, on an expedition that stopped at San Pedro Springs and the San Antonio River, a location they found ideal for a mission. In the following years, Fr. Olivares traveled to Spain to recruit missionaries, and then returned to Mission San Francisco de Solano. In late 1716, he traveled to Mexico City to confer with the new Viceroy, Don Baltazar de Zúñiga, Marqués de Valero, who granted final approval to Olivares' plan to establish a mission north of the Rio Grande (thus the origin of the *de Valero* in the new mission's name).

In February 1718 an expedition under Don Martín de Alarcón, governor of Coahuila and now governor of Texas as well, crossed the Rio Grande. The formal founding of the mission took place 1 May 1718. Four days later, the presidio of San Antonio de Béxar was established nearby. Béxar honored the Duke of Béxar, the Viceroy's brother and a respected Spanish military hero.

The Franciscans brought with them several families of Christianized Indians from Mission San Francisco Solano on the Rio Grande, and used them to help bring the apparently reluctant Indians from the Payaya and Pamaya groups into Mission San Antonio.

The site of the mission was changed several times during its early history. Its final location at today's Alamo Plaza was chosen in 1724 after the original structures were destroyed by a storm. Changes of location were not unusual in the establishment of missions. Sometimes it took living and working at a particular site for a time before drawbacks became evident. By 1720 Mission San Antonio's population stood at 240.

In 1731 the Villa of San Fernando de Béxar was founded near the presidio with the arrival of fifteen families, totaling fifty-five persons, from the Canary Islands. The future San Antonio began to acquire importance as the only Spanish settlement of any size in a very large territory.

Relations between town and mission were not always pleasant. Military authorities often claimed to lack sufficient manpower to post soldiers at each mission. The missionaries argued that the lack of soldiers left them short-handed and unprotected, and that the soldiers were essential to help recover runaways and seek new converts. The missionaries prevailed, and by 1731 there were two soldiers posted at missions San Antonio and San José, and three apiece at the other three missions.

A church was constructed at the mission, probably of adobe, to replace the thatched structure that had been in use for several years, but it collapsed, more than likely because of faulty construction. Work on the stone church known today as The Alamo was begun in 1744, but a storm severely damaged the structure. Although reconstruction began immediately (the keystone bears the date 1758), the building was unfinished when the mission was secularized in 1793.

The Alamo facade and plaza.

Detail from the "Plan of the town of San Antonio, 1730," by Joseph de Villaseñor.

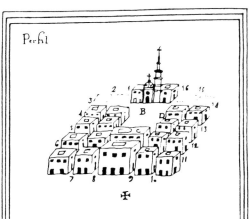

MISSION SAN JOSÉ Y SAN MIGUEL DE AGUAYO. In 1719, while taking refuge from the French at Mission San Antonio, East Texas missionary Fr. Antonio Margil de Jesús of the College of Zacatecas found three Indian bands—the Pampopas, Suliajames, and Pastias—who expressed an interest in joining a new mission. They would not join the one already established at San Antonio because they regarded the Indians there as enemies. With an abundance of unconverted Indians in the area, Fr. Margil decided to establish a halfway support station for the East Texas missions of the Zacatecas friars, just as the Querétaro friars had done with Mission San Antonio.

He drafted a proposal for this new mission on 26 December 1719, and sent it to the Marqués Don José de San Miguel de Aguayo, the new governor of Coahuila and Texas. In his letter, Fr. Margil emphasized the founding of the mission could take place at once, since he had rescued as much church property as he could from East Texas, and this property was now in San Antonio. Some of it could be used for the new foundation.

The governor's decree arrived in about a month, unusually quick for those frontier circumstances. Fr. Olivares at Mission San Antonio objected to the new foundation. In a petition to the governor, he said the Indian bands envisioned for this new mission were enemies of those at his mission and of other nearby bands. This enemy presence would stand in the way of Christianizing the nearby bands, who could conceivably be brought in, since they spoke the same language as the Indians already at Mission San Antonio. His intervention, said Fr. Olivares, stemmed "from a sense of justice and not from malice." Nonetheless, he reminded the authorities that the laws of Castile, as they applied to New Spain and other Spanish territories in America, required a distance of three leagues (about eight miles) in every direction between missions.

The site for the mission was selected immediately, and was described by Lt. Gen. Juan Valdés, who represented the civil authorities at the founding:

> The land offered rich pastures with plentiful wood for beams, stones for making hearths, and fire-wood [sic]. There are excellent exits and entrances along the river for cattle, sheep, goats, and horses. We considered a slight elevation that is very even and spacious to be the best for building the church and pueblo.

Formal ceremonies marked the foundation on 23 February 1720. The missionaries and their new community traced a two-mile acequia, and outlined a mission square of 120 varas (about 334 feet) per side. They named the new foundation Mission San José de San Miguel de Aguayo de Buena Vista (Mission San José of San Miguel de Aguayo of Buena Vista), in honor of the governor. Over the years, popular usage has changed the name to Mission San José **y** San Miguel de Aguayo (Mission San José **and** St. Michael de Aguayo), thus giving the church and mission two patron saints. The Marqués de Aguayo himself visited the new mission in April 1721, and found 227 Indians living there.

By 1724 the new mission was prospering: the acequia was completed and the corn crops yielded a surplus. According to a report of 1727, more Indians were living in the

Seventeenth-century Spanish leaf-shaped lance point.

two San Antonio River missions than in all six of the East Texas missions. Between 1724 and 1727, however, the missionaries decided to abandon Mission San José's first site, on the east bank of the San Antonio River, and move to a new one on the west bank, slightly north of its present location.

The first permanent buildings at the present site were begun during the 1740s. By 1749 there was a friary next to the church, described by Fr. Antonio Ignacio Ciprián to the Zacatecan headquarters as having "a serrated cloister and a porter's office," as well as a granary. The Indian quarters were strongly built of stone, and arranged to make the mission a fortress. Apaches did not dare attack the fortified mission compound directly, although they raided the outlying mission fields and ranches.

When Fr. Gaspar José Solís visited in 1768, the year construction of a stone church began, the mission had a population of 350 Indians. Among the men, 110 could handle weapons for the mission's defense: 45 could use guns and 75 could handle bow and arrow, lance, and other weapons. Education was well advanced, Fr. Solís observed:

> All the mission Indians speak Spanish, except those who were too old when they arrived from the wilderness. Most of them are able to play an instrument: some the guitar, others the violin or the harp. On certain holidays, they sing the rosary in four-voice harmony and accompany themselves with their instruments. All

RAIDERS FROM THE PLAINS All of the missions suffered periodically from Apache attacks. Even Mission San Antonio, which was closest to the presidio and the civilian settlement, was not spared. A report sent to the Viceroy from San Antonio in July 1744 attributes the community's stymied growth to frequent Apache assaults.

> The camp these Indians occupy is about 20 leagues [52 miles] north of the presidio [in the Hill Country], and from there they sally forth to attack the mentioned Presidio of San Antonio de Béxar from all directions, and even to penetrate the Province of Coahuila. They use horses, firearms, and [bows and] arrows with great agility and skill, being unintimidated by the campaigns which were carried out against them in the years of 1732 and '34. They sue for peace when they see themselves threatened, but break it with treachery and deceit, committing murder and all kinds of barbarous atrocities, caring less for their children and wives than for the chance of acquiring a few horses.

Hostilities with Apaches ended around mid-century, when they came under increasing pressure from Comanches and other Indians from the north, and finally accepted a peace with the Spanish. The Lipan Apaches in particular became regular visitors to San Antonio, and eventually a mission was established for them at the San Saba River in 1757. This mission was totally destroyed the following year by a coalition of the Apaches' Indian enemies.

From the 1770s on, the royal government sought to reach an agreement with the Comanches and their allies, a policy which finally led to a peace treaty in 1785. By the 1790s Comanche visitors to San Antonio were common as Apaches.

Lipan Apache Indian, ca. 1850s.

Mission San José y San
Miguel de Aguayo.

ABOVE—Detail of Saint
Joseph, part of the
church's ornate facade.

The shell motif appears in
many aspects of mission
architecture.

20

can sing and dance like civilized people elsewhere, and all have
two outfits: one for everyday work, and a better one for holidays
and celebrations. . . . Boys and girls attend school.

The new mission compound was square, 220 varas (611 feet) on each side, with
two towers on diagonal corners, and entrances on each side. The mission fields were
so productive that San José could supply its own needs and still send produce to the
other San Antonio missions, the nearby presidio, and other presidios in East Texas.
Crops grown included corn, beans, lentils, melons, watermelons, peaches, potatoes,
sweet potatoes, and sugarcane. The peaches, in particular, sometimes weighed nearly
a pound each.

Cattle, horses, and other animals were raised at the mission's Rancho El Atascoso,
located 10–12 leagues (26–31 miles) south between today's Pleasanton and Poteet,
Texas. The stock included fifteen hundred head of cattle, five thousand sheep and
goats, about ten herds of mares, and four of asses. All this was run exclusively with
Indian labor.

The stone church at Mission San José was nearing completion in 1777 and was
described by Fr. Juan Agustín Morfi, who accompanied the newly appointed Comman-
dant General Teodoro de Croix on his inspection tour of the frontier areas of New
Spain. Morfi, who visited all the other frontier missions during his journey, said
Mission San José was

> . . . in truth, the first mission in America, not in point of time,
> but in point of beauty, plan, and strength, so that there is not
> a presidio [sic] along the entire frontier line that can compare
> with it.

It is based on this statement that San José has been called the "Queen of the Missions."
Morfi continued:

> The whole structure is admirably proportioned and strongly built
> of stone and mortar, chiefly of a sandy limestone that is light and
> porous when freshly quarried but in a few days hardens and
> becomes one with the mortar.
> . . . This stone is obtained from a quarry near the Mission of
> Nuestra Señora de la Concepción.

Morfi was very impressed by the church's ornate facade with its statues
and flat surface ornamentation. Of the well-known "Rose Window," the
exterior frame of the sacristy's south window, Morfi says nothing; it was
apparently added after the completion of the church in 1782. The "Rose
Window" is traditionally credited to Pedro Huízar, who was listed in the
mission's records as a *carpintero*, or carpenter.

Indian quarters lined the
walls of the compound.

MISSION NUESTRA SEÑORA DE LA PURÍSIMA CONCEPCIÓN DE ACUÑA. In 1716, near the Angelina River in today's Nacogdoches County, Mission Nuestra Señora de la Purísima Concepción was founded to work with the Ainay, a band of the Tejas Indians. A presidio was established nearby. The Tejas traditionally lived in small, scattered villages, and bringing them into a mission proved impossible. After a couple of years of fruitless work and great hardship, the missionaries were forced to leave the area when the French threatened in 1719.

The mission was re-established in 1721, but again the results were poor. In March 1731 the Viceroy approved a petition to re-establish it and other East Texas Queretaran missions along the San Antonio River.

Church furnishings and other supplies along with herds of cattle, horses, mules, and burros were driven 375 miles west. Upon arrival, the missionaries and soldiers immediately began to gather Indians. They managed to recruit about one thousand, whom they divided among the three new missions.

The name Mission Concepción was retained for the new foundation, but this time it was called Nuestra Señora de la Purísima Concepción de Acuña, in honor of the current Viceroy of New Spain, Don Juan de Acuña.

By the end of 1740 the mission was apparently doing well, but still operated with temporary buildings.

This painting on the library ceiling is commonly known as the "eye of God."

Cross and religious medal from the late 1700s.

Soon thereafter construction of stone buildings began. Reports by Fr. Francisco Xavier Ortiz over the next seventeen years document the mission's progress. By 1745 a stone wall had been built around the mission complex. Inside that wall were a two-story house for the missionaries, three houses for the soldiers, and a large granary. Indian quarters, however, were still jacales. A new church was under construction and was half-finished. The mission's acequia originated at a stone dam that had been constructed in the south section of the San Antonio River's loop in what is today downtown San Antonio, ran through the mission compound, and rejoined the river below Mission San José's dam.

The completed church was dedicated on 8 December 1755. It had the shape of a cross, and was some 32 varas (about 89 feet) long and 8 varas (about 22 feet) wide in the nave, and 17 varas (47¼ feet) wide at the transept. Its walls, 45 inches thick, were made of adobe mixed with small stones, with a facing of dressed stone. The church had two bell towers and a portal of carved stone, with a niche above the door containing a statue of the Virgin. Fr. Ortiz reported that the moon was painted on one side, and the sun on the other, and that the entire facade was painted with geometric "flower work." The arch above the door bore the following inscription:

A SU PATRONA Y PRINCESSA
CON ESTAS ARMAS, ATIENDE
ESTA MISSION, Y DEFIENDE
EL PUNTO DE SU PUREZA

"This mission honors its Patroness and Princess, and defends with these arms the doctrine of Her Purity."

The 1762 report of Fr. Ortiz describes Mission Concepción as a productive operation. The granary contained 800 *fanegas* (about 1,280 bushels) of corn and 50 fanegas (about 80 bushels) of beans, and the mission farm had 45 yokes of oxen. The mission ranch, Rancho El Pasthle, maintained 200 mares and 110 horses, 610 head of cattle, and 2,200 sheep and goats. The ranch, located about 12 leagues (31 miles) east of the mission, had stone quarters for the Indian vaqueros and their families. But all was not well. The total population of the mission had declined to 207. The remote ranch was abandoned in 1767 because of Indian raids.

Mission Nuestra Señora de la Purísima Concepción.

Painted decorations can be seen in the convento.

The painted facade of Mission Concepción as rendered by Ernst Schuchard in the 1930s.

A RIOT OF COLOR Mexico's colonial architecture inherited a rich tradition from Spain. It mixed the classical lines of the Renaissance with the extravagantly rich decoration of the Moors. Mudéjar architecture, a marriage of styles and tastes produced by Moorish artists and craftspeople working for Christian patrons, was very influential.

Texas frontier mission architecture reflected Mexico's interpretation of the styles of Spain. But the mission builders had to work with materials available in an isolated region with a sparse population. The craftspeople who helped construct the missions were imported artisans who were willing to brave hardships on the frontier and work with Indian laborers.

The missions today may appear monochromatically drab, but in their day they were riotously colorful. We get a hint of this in Fr. Morfi's description of Mission San José in 1778.

> It has a beautiful cupola, though it is overcrowded with unnecessary ornaments. The facade is very costly because of the statues and ornaments with which it is heavily decorated, detracting somewhat from its natural beauty. In a word, no one could have imagined that there were such good artists in so desolate a place.

Only traces of this decoration remain today, but the records abound with references to it. Early photographs from 1858–60 clearly show the designs on the facades of the missions. The first artist to have visually documented these decorations, however, was probably Edward Everett, who came to San Antonio with the United States Army during the Mexican War in 1846. In his watercolors of Mission Concepción, Everett clearly showed what remained of the painted facade and the towers.

A travel account of San Antonio by William Corner, published in 1890, contains the following descriptions:

Of Missions Concepción and San José:
The front of Mission Concepción must have been very gorgeous with color, for it was frescoed all over with red and blue quatrefoil crosses of different pattern and with large yellow and orange squares to simulate great dressed stones. This frescoing is rapidly disappearing, and from a little distance the front looks to be merely gray with undecorated stone. The baptistry walls are frescoed with weird looking designs, dim and faded, of the Crucifixion and Los Dolores. . . . [At San José] the front was frescoed in red blue and yellow in a pretty design, but this is now very difficult to discern.

In the 1930s Ernst Schuchard, an engineer with Pioneer Flour Mills in San Antonio, made a thorough study of the mission decorations. Examining traces of designs in the plaster at missions San José and Concepción showed there was nothing haphazard about them. Everything was laid out with rule and compass, and most outlines were cut into the mortar with a sharp-pointed instrument.

Schuchard did a chemical analysis of the pigments and found only four definite colors remaining: red, yellow, black, and blue, all made from readily available local materials. He also found sources that talked about pigments being mixed with milk for application. What amazed Schuchard most was the permanence of these colors. The designs yielded only to the destruction of plaster surfaces or to the application of whitewash. Once the whitewash was removed, the colors could be found underneath, still strong and clear.

What is left of the ancient decoration at the missions today is but a trace of what once was there. In 1988 a team of experts, using the same techniques used to restore and clean the Sistine Chapel in Rome, cleaned and restored the remaining painted surfaces at the missions. While working on the so-called "God's eye" room or library at Mission Concepción, the team discovered that the single eye visible for years was actually part of a mustachioed "sun face." They were also able to restore the original painted decorative scheme on the walls of that room.

Schuchard's vision of the original painted facade of the church at Mission San José.

MISSION SAN JUAN CAPISTRANO.

Predecessor to Mission San Juan Capistrano was the East Texas Mission San José de los Nazonis, founded in 1716 for the Nazoni and Nadaco Indians, in what is today Nacogdoches County. The original mission was abandoned in 1719 and reopened in 1721. Its missionaries finally came to the San Antonio River with the other Querétaran fathers in 1731. Mission San Juan was founded on the east bank of the river at the site it still occupies, seven miles from today's downtown San Antonio.

Progress did not come easily to the two smaller missions, San Juan and Espada. San Juan was about three miles away from San José, and Espada was about four miles distant. Isolation made them vulnerable to Indian raids. Although Apaches would not attack the mission compounds, traveling to and from the missions was dangerous. The situation was complicated by the dispute between the missions and the civil authorities over stationing soldiers at the missions.

In fact, Indians at Mission San Juan seemed more rebellious than most, and in 1737 more than two hundred, including about ninety already baptized, simply left the mission and returned to the wilderness. Some came back six months later, but the rest never returned.

The reports of Fr. Ortiz from 1745, 1756, and 1762 show slow progress. By 1756 the original thatch-roofed chapel had been replaced by a stone building with a roof supported by hewn wood beams. Indian housing had been upgraded to adobe houses with roofs thatched with hay or grass by 1762. Construction was started on a larger church, but the building was never finished.

Mission San Juan
Capistrano.

Details of ironwork.

"Mission San Juan"
painted by Herman
Lungkwitz in 1851.

The gate to the com-
pound at Mission San
Juan.

MISSION SAN FRANCISCO DE LA ESPADA. Mission Espada is traced back to other missions founded with San Francisco as their patron saint. The first was Mission San Francisco de los Tejas, established in 1690 near the Neches River in present-day Houston County. The second was Mission Nuestro Padre San Francisco de los Tejas, established in 1716 about ten miles east of the previous site. Neither of these was successful; the second one was abandoned in 1719 because of the French threat.

In 1721, when the missionaries returned to East Texas from San Antonio, a third mission was established on the same site as the second one and named Mission San Francisco de los Neches. In 1729 mission work among the Neches, a band of the Tejas, ceased, and the remaining church property was moved to the San Antonio River and used to found Mission San Francisco de la Espada on 5 March 1731. (No definite explanation exists for the de la Espada designation.)

Mission Espada, located on the west side of the river, was the farthest from town. Its location left it more exposed than Mission San Juan to Apache attacks and its progress was slow. Only temporary structures existed at the mission until the 1740s.

Like his counterpart at Mission San Juan, Fr. Ignacio Ysasmendi had to contend with rebellious Indians at Espada. In January 1737 he reported that an Indian had refused to be punished for breaking mission rules, and was joined by others in threatening the priest. Under the circumstances, the priest had to let the Indian go unpunished, which undermined his authority. Two months later, in April, the Tacame Indians at the mission ran away, and in June the remaining Indians also left the mission. Of 230 converted Indians, not one stayed behind.

The missionary's messages, promising forgiveness if the runaways returned, went unheeded. Finally, in December, an expedition of ten soldiers and the missionary traveled into Apache territory, where the Indians had taken refuge, and the priest convinced 108 of them to return. The Tacame, however, never came back.

The 1745 report of Fr. Ortiz says the sacristy of a planned stone church had been completed, and the room was being used for church services. In 1756 the mission church was finished. By the time of Fr. Ortiz's report in 1762, a larger stone church had been started. This second church was never completed because the stone available nearby was poor.

Eighteenth-century santo, possibly Saint Francis of Assisi.

Unique doorway to the church at Mission Espada.

Mission San Francisco de la Espada.

Kunth evening primroses.

MANUAL
PARA ADMINISTRAR
LOS SANTOS SACRAMENTOS
DE PENITENCIA,
EUCHARISTIA, EXTREMA-UNCION,
Y MATRIMONIO:
DAR GRACIAS DESPUES DE COMULGAR,
Y AYUDAR A BIEN MORIR

A los Indios de las Naciones: Pajalates, Orejones,
Pacaos, Pacóas, Tilijayas, Alafapas, Pauſanes, y otras
muchas diferentes, que ſe hallan en las Miſſiones del
Rio de San Antonio, y Rio Grande, pertenecientes
à el Colegio de la Santiſſima Cruz de la Ciudad de
Queretaro, como ſon: Los Pacuàches, Meſcàles,
Pampôpas, Tàcames, Chayopînes, Venados, Pamà-
ques, y toda la Juventud de Pihuiques, Borrados,
Sanipaos, y Manos de Perro.

COMPUESTO
POR EL P. Fr. BARTHOLOME GARCIA,
Predicador Apoſtolico, y actual Miſſionero de la
Miſſion de N. S. P. S. Francifco de dicho Colegio,
y Rio de San Antonio, en la Provincia
de Texas.

Impreſſo con las Licencias neceſſarias en la Imprenta de los Herederos de
Doña Maria de Rivera, en la Calle de San Bernardo, y eſquina de la Plazuela
de el Volador. Año de 1760.

Title page of the *Manual para Administrar los Santos Sacramentos de Penitencia, Eucharista, Extrema Unción, y Matrimonio,* 1760.

Life at the missions. Daily mission life was regulated by the mission bell, which called the community to Mass, prayers, church feasts, and other religious observances, and was used to sound alarms. A 1760 manual of operations from Mission Concepción detailed at length when to toll the bell, what feasts to observe during the year and how to observe them, when to have processions and how to organize them, and on what days to dispense with prayers. Two mission women were required to sweep the church and sacristy regularly. The new missionary was instructed to send church linens to the presidio for washing and mending, because no one at the mission could do that properly.

The mission Indian population had a system of self-government that paralleled Spanish local government. Former chiefs or elders were given special positions of authority, and responsibility for some discipline was placed in Indian hands rather than in those of the priest. Authority alternated between leaders of the various Indian groups represented in the mission. Some Indian leaders were elected by voice vote of the men, while others were selected by the missionary. This internal governing system was not true self-government; it was rather like the election of officers among primary school students. The system helps to explain how a couple of missionaries and a couple of soldiers could make an orderly village out of a gathering of a few hundred natives, some of whom might have been traditional enemies.

At the head was the *gobernador,* or governor; other officers were the *alcalde,* or mayor, *justicia,* or justice, and *regimiento,* a term related to the noun *regidor,* or council member. No document explains exactly what the duties of the Indian officials were, but a law from 1618 states that the Indian alcalde could investigate, arrest, and bring delinquents to the local Spanish jail. He could also administer punishments of one day's incarceration or six to eight lashes to Indians who missed Mass, got drunk, or committed similar offenses.

At the founding of Mission San Antonio, provincial governor Don Martín de Alarcón named Santiago Ximenes, one of the highest chiefs of the Jarame, gobernador. He also appointed other high chiefs of the Indians represented at the mission to other positions. At Mission Concepción, it was customary to select the gobernador and alcalde in alternate years from among the Pajalache and Tacame, two groups living there. Indian officials were sworn into office in the name of the King, and the gobernador received a staff as symbol of his position. He and other officials also were granted special items of clothing as tokens of their office.

Two other important positions, those of *fiscal* and *mayordomo,* had combined civil and religious duties and were selected by the missionary. The fiscal (a term today denoting either a representative of the treasury or a district attorney) was caretaker of the mission church. He kept the baptismal font filled with Holy Water, burned palms for Ash Wednesday, made sure Indians attended classes, and appointed and supervised women who swept the church and made tortillas for the friars' refectory. He doled out soap to women on Saturdays; parceled out rations of tobacco, meat, corn, and salt; and distributed melons or other fruit in season, making sure to gather the seeds for replanting. He was also in charge of distributing treats of chocolate or *piloncillo* (brown sugar cones) on special holidays or celebrations.

The mayordomo selected Indians to portray Apostles during the Easter celebration and supervised preparations for the feast of Corpus Christi. More significantly, he was in charge of some of the most important mission laborers: *bueyeros*, or ox drivers, who took mission cows and oxen to and from the pasture each day; vaqueros who worked mission livestock, and the *caporal*, or ranch foreman, who helped the vaqueros bring in cattle to be slaughtered each weekend. The mayordomo also supervised *pastores*, or shepherds, who tended flocks of sheep and goats; farmhands who worked mission fields; and the *obrajero*, or shop foreman, who supervised the mission shops, including cotton processing and wool carding and spinning. The 1760 manual instructs the new missionary that

> the mayordomo's office is permanent and only for grave reasons can the incumbent be deposed. But in case of removal or death, the missionary may appoint one who is well suited to the task, always being careful that the Indian whom he appoints should be one of the most intelligent among the Spanish speakers, who is able to command and to carry out orders. It would not be out of order to consult privately with those Indians who can give him advice in a disinterested way.

Foodstuffs, tobacco, and salt were apportioned weekly according to an established scale: so much for women with a family and so much for those who were widowed or lived alone. The missionaries gave supplementary rations towards the end of week, however, if necessary. In times of scarcity or drought, portions were reduced for all. The mission Indians' diet was very similar to that of people of modest means in Mexico today. For breakfast they had *atole*, a thin, milky gruel made mostly from cornmeal. Their more substantial meal was *pozole*, a soup or stew made with meat, corn, beans or lentils, and vegetables. The diet of the missionaries was not much different: mostly soups and stews with a few different ingredients. Indians supplemented their mission diet with plants, berries, roots, and other familiar foods from pre-mission days. Archeological evidence also shows mission Indians hunted, prepared, and consumed various game.

The 1760 manual notes that missionaries had to be vigilant to regulate contact between mission Indians and presidio personnel and townspeople, to prevent the Indians from being cheated or abused. Missionaries distributed two twists of tobacco to adult men and women after Sunday mass. Any remaining tobacco was returned to the missionary, who could give more to those who requested some later in the week. No extra tobacco was given out before Wednesday. Otherwise the Indians would be tempted to squander what they received on Sunday, bartering it for trifles with the people at the presidio.

Captain Toribio Urrutia's report of 1740 to the Viceroy mentions an

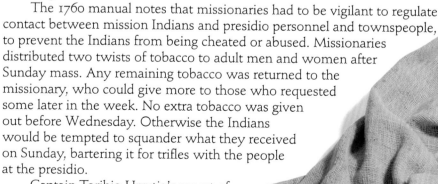

Thimbles and cotton cloth from the mission period.

order to have mission Indians parcelled out among the Canary Islanders in town to work for them, repartimiento-style. Captain Urrutia warned such a policy would drive mission Indians back to the wilderness, and that this would weaken the missions. These Indians would surely tell their unconverted brethren about being forced to serve the Spaniards, and that would make them even more resistant to conversion. Authorities must have listened, for not only was this policy rescinded, but Spanish settlers were subsequently prohibited from even hiring mission Indians.

The Espada dam was an integral part of the acequia system that irrigated the missions' fields.

Some cotton and woolen clothing and blankets for mission Indians were provided from the mission's workshops. The 1760 manual contains lengthy instructions about how to provide clothing for both men and women. Married women were to make the clothes for their husbands and children; clothing for single men was made for them. The supply trains that came from Mexico once or twice a year brought, among other things, shoes and hats, plus ribbons, beads, necklaces, and earrings for the women.

Aside from their role in providing protection, soldiers sometimes helped missionaries train Indians and taught them simplified military drills. In addition, skilled Spanish craftspeople—saddle makers, candle makers, blacksmiths, stonemasons, carpenters, and women who made biscuits and bread—handled tasks for which mission Indians had not yet been trained. The population of the frontier areas was sparse, so there were never many such craftspeople available. When exceptional skills were required, such as for the construction of churches, master craftsmen were brought in under contract.

Mission agriculture depended on irrigation, so cleaning acequias and maintaining bridges and dams was a major annual chore. All tasks of an agricultural society had to be carried out: preparing fields, planting, weeding, repairing fences, gathering and bringing in the harvest. When the harvest was abundant, it was customary to decorate the last wagonload and bring it back to the mission with singing and rejoicing. At such times, the missionary would treat all to a bit of wine. The last feast of the year would be Christmas Eve and Christmas Day, when the Indians would do the dance of the matachines. On Christmas Day, the dance would also be performed at the presidio, the governor's house, and other places in the settlement.

The total population of the San Antonio missions was not very large, never exceeding four hundred persons at any one of them, and seldom surpassing three hundred. The numbers fluctuated, increasing when Indian groups in the area were under heaviest pressure, and declining at times such as the epidemic of 1739, which killed scores of mission Indians and drove many survivors away. By 1775 mission populations were in irreversible decline.

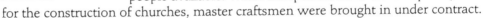

Conversion or coercion? Mission Indian life often has been presented in idyllic terms. For example, the translator of a San Antonio missions document states:

> The Indians were like little children and did not assume responsibility easily. But the kind missionaries sought to train them so that they could help in managing the affairs of the mission.

This image is reminiscent of descriptions of the old slave-holding South, where supposedly-childlike slaves were merely objects of a system to which they offered little resistance, despite the back-breaking toil and abuse. These racist images persisted until more critical historical evaluation began to be applied to that period of American history, and a more realistic picture of African slaves as full personalities began to emerge.

Imagine being thrust into a totally foreign cultural, linguistic, and religious environment, forced to adapt without any preparation for the change, and without a support system to ease the transition. It would not be easy.

Consider the Indians who were brought into the missions. They were expected to abandon their culture and adopt another one. They had to give up their native language and learn a European one, not related in any way to their own. They had to live in a community where all communication took place in that new language, foreign to all except to the missionaries and the soldiers. And there was another foreign language in the equation: Latin used in religious services.

They had to accept a new religion with a complicated theology and a world view totally unrelated to anything they had known. Everything they had learned—about life and the world, about how to be a human being—had to be cast aside.

This "cultural divestment" required abandoning everything that had shaped the individual's life: material culture; songs, dances, stories; even family arrangements, since some Indian groups practiced polygamy, an arrangement the new culture did not

Engraving of Indians digging irrigation ditches.

tolerate. A man with multiple wives was expected to choose one and marry her. Sexual mores, in general, were quite different in the new society. Near-nudity that had been considered natural and normal was condemned by the friars, and Indians had to learn to wear and be comfortable in clothes made of new and strange materials.

In the new setting, the Indians also had to give up their nomadic habits, become part of a sedentary community, and get used to a different pace of life. People whose lives had been ruled by the seasons and by the need to find food and shelter now had to adapt to a strictly regimented life that probably took some time to comprehend. In their hunting-gathering society, approximately twenty-three hours a week was spent on acquiring food, and this provided an adequate diet.

At the mission, work and religious obligations began in the early morning and ended in the evening. Mardith Schuetz, in a study on mission Indians says:

> The most important adjustment may have been to something called "time": waking, eating, attending catechism or mass, working, playing, and sleeping [at specific times]. For a people who hunted or gathered when there was nothing left to eat, who ate, slept, or loved as the mood struck, routine had to be artificial.

Scheduled work was also new to mission Indians, whether it involved laboring in the fields, tending cattle and dealing with horses, shepherding sheep and goats, or learning a craft. How could a hunter be made to understand that the mission herds he tended were not for eating when hunger struck, but for use in the future?

The missionaries tended to look upon the Indians as children who could be molded to the will and ways of a parent figure. But reducciones were not always voluntary: the fathers went with soldiers to bring in Indians for the founding of missions, and made trips to round up unconverted ones when mission populations declined. A 1765 report from an inspection trip by Fr. Francisco Xavier Ortiz explains:

> The horses and other beasts [of burden] at the missions are used
> to bring in runaway Indians, [to carry] the missionaries [when
> they] go out accompanied by Spanish-speaking Indians to look
> for unconverted Indians, and to tend the mission herds.

Soldiers assigned to protect the missions represented Spanish authority, which could clearly be coercive. Fray Romualdo Cartagena of the College of Querétaro stated:

> It is seen everyday that in missions where there are no soldiers,
> there is no success, for the Indians, being children of fear, are
> more strongly appealed to by the glistening of the sword than by
> the voice of five missionaries. . . . For the spiritual and temporal
> progress of the missions, two soldiers are needed, for the Indians
> cannot be trusted, especially in new conversions.

Indians resisted the new way of life in a variety of ways. Many fled to open country, either to resume their previous life, to join brethren who had refused to be brought into the system, or, in extreme cases, to join the Apaches. Documents are full of references to this constant running away.

Desire for the old ways was strong for many mission Indians: the number of runaways increased during the times of year when traditional mitotes were held. A report by Fr. Gaspar José Solís dated 1767–68 said "whenever the priests are not paying attention, the Indian men and women slip away to the woods to their mitotes and to dance with the pagan Indians." He adds that "this practice is very much guarded against, and those who are caught in it are severely punished."

Indians who accepted Christianity did not understand that their conversion was a binding contract in the eyes of the church and the Spanish civil authorities. Runaways and those who participated in the mitotes were breaking that contract, thus becoming apostates: people who rejected the faith after having accepted it. Church and state in Spain did not deal lightly with apostates.

The *cepo*, or stock, and *grillos*, or leg irons, were used in some missions by the gobernadores and alcaldes to punish— with the approval of the missionaries—those most stubborn

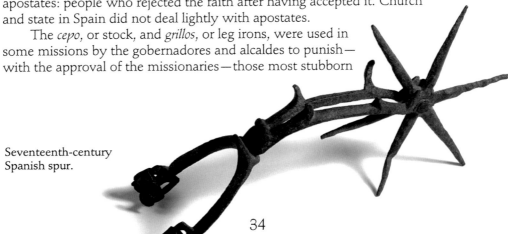

Seventeenth-century
Spanish spur.

and given to escaping. Spaniards from town who gambled with Indians or bartered trinkets for their clothes were to be be tied to a post and whipped.

Resistance to the life and rule of the mission could take other forms. Missionaries complained about the laziness and unreliability of the Indians, the need to supervise them constantly, the ease with which they broke or lost tools and other items, and their tendency to gamble away or trade what they had been given, including their clothes. Some of this behavior was undoubtedly rooted in dissatisfaction.

Serious trauma does not need to be physical. Mental trauma and stress can also cause illness and death, and mission Indians were under tremendous pressure. It did not take epidemics to kill Indians at the missions. Scholars analyzing the records conclude that their health was not very good to begin with.

A 1762 report observed that Indians suffered from a variety of illnesses. It was not unusual for entire "nations" to perish without any individual ever reaching old age, and that even a relatively light illness could often be fatal. It also notes a high incidence of infant mortality. The Father Visitor blamed this on the Indians' excesses: they did not protect themselves from bad weather; and they refused to maintain the diets, purges, sweats, and other cures prescribed by the missionaries. He also observed that the missions would be totally empty, or at least severely depopulated, were it not for the constant efforts of the missionary fathers to bring in new, unconverted groups.

Despite the constant influx of the unconverted, the San Antonio missions never were able to balance deaths with births, and the eventual disappearance of an unconverted population played a role in the closing of the missions. Even before that, mission life was not all happy Indians and kindly missionaries, singing hymns of praise.

Decline and secularization. Missionaries from the College of Querétaro turned over their San Antonio missions to the College of Zacatecas in 1773. Even then, and certainly by the time Fr. Morfi visited in 1777, the missions were declining rapidly.

The growing importance of the civilian settlement of San Fernando aggravated long-standing conflicts. Local citizens coveted the vast land holdings of the missions, and merchants and entrepreneurs resented the economic competition of mission enterprises. By 1780 one of the missionaries expressed his frustration:

> Everything, everything is turned around. There are few Indians
> and many hired hands. There are few cattle, and even so, no one
> to sell them to because there are too many grazers. Even if the
> missions had an abundance of corn, there are too many farmers,
> so many that some have abandoned agriculture. The resources
> that sustained the missions have [now] been reduced.

With increased development in the frontier areas, the interests and the policies of the colonial administration changed. The success of colonial settlements made the missions obsolete, since many of their original purposes had been achieved.

By 1792 even the missionaries advocated secularization. In a 7 September report,

Fr. José Francisco López, the Father President of the Texas missions, suggested that Mission San Antonio be completely secularized. The residents of that mission were well-instructed Christians, mostly children of Indian fathers and Spanish mothers. Fr. López pointed out there were no more pagan Coahuiltecans within a radius of 150 miles.

The Father President also proposed that secular affairs of the other four missions be put in the hands of officials appointed by the government, that resident missionaries be assigned to two of the missions, and the other two be reduced to *visitas*, or subordinate congregations.

Mission San Antonio was secularized in 1793. The spiritual care of the people who remained was assigned to the pastor of the Spaniards in the town of San Fernando across the river. The following year, the other four were partially secularized, with Mission Concepción assigned to a missionary living at San José, and Mission San Juan to a friar residing at Espada. These two missionaries were exempted from all administration of temporal matters; they would function, in effect, as ordinary parish priests.

The decrees issued in 1794 regulated the inventory of mission land, animals, and goods and their partitioning among the remaining mission Indians. The Indians were "to possess the same complete liberty that is granted by the laws to Spaniards and other races termed rational," and authorities were enjoined to make sure that the Indians were paid just prices for their goods and their products and just wages for their labor. Gamblers or peddlers of alcoholic beverages were specifically prohibited from entering what were to become Indian pueblos, lest they corrupt the Indians, leaving them tempted to resort to thievery to feed themselves and their families.

After the mission lands were surveyed, a specific portion of the best land was to be set aside as common land, to be worked by all for the benefit of the Indian community. The remaining land was to be divided among the Indians in equal portions, and titles of ownership were to be issued, containing accurate descriptions of each property. The Indians were not to be permitted to "alienate, sublease, or mortgage their land in any way, not even for pious purposes," and they were obligated to keep their apportionment cultivated and in good condition. Anyone who neglected the land two years in a row was liable to have it confiscated and given to "someone else who is a more industrious and steady worker."

Secularization was complete by 1823.

These decrees notwithstanding, Fr. López expressed little faith in the mission Indians' ability to prosper under the new arrangements.

It is certain that as soon as the Indians receive the goods [from the division of the mission's property], they will misuse them, sell them, and give them to the Spaniards, and by using their small patrimony in games, drunkenness, and other vices, they will want more when they return to the house of their Father missionary, asking for help to alleviate their hunger and to clothe them; and when the poor missionary will have to dismiss them from his door in sorrow, not being able to help them sufficiently, even by sharing with them the bread of his own sustenance, he will have to practice patience, charity, and compassion, and will see many of his poor Indians go hungry,

naked, and dejected, and exposed to serve the Spaniards to get
food. But since these are the consequences that will follow from
transfering the goods to their awkward management and miscon-
duct, they are also unavoidable conditions which keep the Indian
in the natural sphere with all the rest of them. This is neither
surprising to the Indians, nor is it proper for the apostolic institute
to strive to suspend the course of divine providence, which in its
hidden design maintains all the natives of this America in the
condition of the most lowly, humble, poor, and abject men.

There were 102 persons living at Mission San José at the time of secularization.
Among the converted Indians were 27 men, 26 women, 11 boys, 14 girls, and 6
widows. Those who had not yet been converted included one neophyte leader with
his wife and daughter, 6 men, 5 women, a boy, and 3 girls. Both Christian and
unconverted Indians received land.

The mission communities continued to limp along for another two decades, but
Spanish residents became increasingly prominent, either by renting property or simply
as *arrimados*, or squatters. In the colonial society of that period, the designation
"Spanish" was not necessarily a racial one, but rather a cultural one. Persons of mixed
race who were culturally integrated into the society were considered Spanish.

By 1805 the alcaldes at all the missions were considered Spanish. An 1809 report
from Mission San José stated that no deeds for the individually assigned land parcels
had been given to the supposed owners and that no document had been found giving
the exact boundaries of the mission. Instead boundaries "accepted by public opinion"
were recorded. An addendum to this report said the alcaldes at the missions were
"Spanish" while the governors were Indians, but that none of them had the qualifica-
tions necessary to properly maintain the property under their care. According to the last
report on the missions in 1815, the community at Mission San José consisted of 109
persons, 49 Indians, and 60 "Spaniards."

The Mexican rebellion against Spain began in September 1810; Mexican independence was proclaimed in 1821. During the early Mexican period, Fr. Refugio de la
Garza, parish priest of San Fernando, represented the province of Texas in the Mexican
National Congress. While there, he became an ardent advocate of complete secularization of the remaining mission lands, large portions of which he subsequently acquired.

On 13 September 1823 the Mexican government ordered the final and complete
secularization of the missions. The following year, on 29 February 1824, Fr. José
Antonio Díaz signed the inventories of what remained, and turned over the four mission churches that today are included in the San Antonio Missions National Historical
Park to a representative of the Bishop of Monterrey. The San Antonio missions were
now under the jurisdiction of the secular clergy.

It did not take long for the mission buildings to fall into disrepair. Without the
guiding presence and authority of the Franciscans, people who remained at the mission
complexes did nothing to maintain the buildings. As early as 1819, four years before
the final secularization decree, damage and decay were reported.

In January 1841 the legislature of the new Republic of Texas passed a law
acknowledging the Catholic Church's ownership of the mission buildings and their
surrounding lands. Recognized ownership, however, did not stop deterioration.

M

ISSION SAN ANTONIO: "THE ALAMO." After secularization, the compound at Mission San Antonio was used to garrison soldiers from the *Segunda Compañía Volante de San Carlos de Parras*, a mobile cavalry unit from Parras, Coahuila, and to house their families. A congregation was established for them, using the former sacristy as a chapel. Apparently, much of the company had been recruited from a small pueblo called El Alamo de Parras, and many now assume that the common appellation of the mission as "El Alamo" stems from this.

"Ruins of the Church of the Alamo" by Edward Everett, 1847.

The Texan revolutionaries were using the mission as a military fort and prison when the famous siege and battle took place from 23 February to 6 March 1836. During the hostilities great damage was done to the structures that remained. An early sketch by Mary Adams Maverick shows that the top of the facade was missing. Watercolors from 1847 by Edward Everett confirm the damage and give a more detailed look at the ruin.

In 1845 the Bishop of San Antonio leased the ruins to the United States Government for use as a military quartermaster depot. To make the building usable, the Army finished the facade and roofed the old mission church. Everett, who was thoroughly familiar with the building, did not appreciate the reconstruction:

> . . . I regret to see by a late engraving of this ruin, tasteless hands
> have evened off the rough walls . . . surmounting them with a
> rediculous [sic] scroll, giving the building the appearance of the
> headboard of a bedstead.

The "rediculous scroll," which so distinguishes the facade today, was meant to disguise a gabled roof the Army had put over the mission.

The Catholic Church sold the surrounding mission property, but retained ownership of the former mission church until 1883, when it was sold for $20,000 to the State of Texas. In 1905 the state entrusted administration of The Alamo to the Daughters of the Republic of Texas, who had become interested in the site and had acquired some of the surrounding property.

MISSION SAN JOSÉ. After the partial secularization of 1794, the number of "Spanish" settlers at Mission San José increased. By the time of the last report on the missions in 1815, the population of 109 included 49 Indians and 60 "Spaniards." Juan Antonio Padilla, in a report dated 1819, says that although the church was already in disrepair, it still had rich ornaments, sacred vases, and silver set with jewels and ornaments. The convento "has a portion that is threatened with ruin, . . . and for the rest [of the buildings], some have fallen down and others are poorly repaired by certain *vecinos agregados* (squatters)." The writer remarked that there were some *castas* (half-castes or mixed-blood people) living there.

After the final secularization decree in 1824, the decay continued. When Edward Everett saw the church in 1846, it was still in use, although "fast going to decay." The roof and some of the architectural details were "covered with a vegetation, much of it flowering," a detail which he included in his drawings, and weather and the action of the roots was rapidly ruining the building. To make matters worse, during the Mexican War of 1846–48 United States troops stationed at the mission entertained themselves by shooting at the facade, aiming particularly for the heads and hands of the statues. According to Everett, the "jekels" (jacales) around the wall, rough stone hovels or completely dilapidated structures, were "inhabited by Mexican families of the lowest class. There were also a few Texans, looking like bandits, occupying the rear buildings."

Between the middle of the nineteenth century and the beginning of the twentieth, damage grew progressively worse. All the buildings except the sacristy became ruins, and the perimeter walls and the Indian houses disappeared. The roofs of the granary and convento collapsed. Finally, a section of the north wall of the church fell in 1868,

Interior of the church of Mission San José looking toward the altar, ca. 1932–33.

ABOVE—Detail of the facade, Lady of Guadalupe.

and the church's dome and most of the roof came tumbling down in 1874. The main doors of the church were stolen between 1880–90.

Serious preservation efforts did not begin until 1917 when the Texas Historic Landmarks Association and the De Zavala Chapter of the Daughters of the Republic of Texas took an interest in the mission. Since then, a host of organizations has taken part in the project. The San Antonio Conservation Society, the "community conscience" where historical preservation is concerned, has been an active participant. The National Society of Colonial Dames in Texas, the Archdiocese of San Antonio, and the County of Bexar also have been involved. In 1934 the Archdiocese signed an agreement with the Federal Government's Work Projects Administration (WPA), one of the Depression-era public works programs, to reconstruct and restore the mission compound at San José. With the exception of the sacristy, convento, and parts of the church walls, what exists today at the mission is reconstructed. Although the historical accuracy of some of this reconstruction might be questioned, it serves to give visitors a good idea of the physical layout of a mission.

In 1941 the entire mission was made a Historic Site within the Texas State Parks system and designated a national historic site, not federally owned. This brought the National Park Service into the administration agreement in an advisory capacity, providing technical assistance for the preservation and use of the site, and paved the way for the eventual establishment of the national historical park.

"Mission La Concepción," an engraving that appeared in *Harper's New Monthly Magazine* in the late 1800s.

MISSION CONCEPCIÓN. The population of Mission Concepción in 1794, when the partial secularization decrees went into effect, was only 38 persons: 16 men, 15 women, a boy, and 6 girls. By then, Concepción was a *visita* of San José. The census of 1809 reported a total population of 53: 32 "Spaniards" and only 21 Indians. The mission was gradually abandoned, and the report of 1815 says that the few parishioners of the congregation attended church services at San José, where the only pastor tending the missions was stationed.

Four years later, Concepción was totally abandoned. Padilla's report of 1819 says that the church

Moorish arch and
stairway connecting the
Father President's office
to the church.

> . . . is in bad condition because of damage by time. It has deteri-
> orated considerably because of the absence of priests and natives.
> The buildings of the convent and the other offices are in the
> worst condition. Of other buildings, there remain only heaps of
> rubbish. This mission has a large irrigating ditch, although not in
> use now. . . . For three years some citizens of Béxar have been
> planting these *labores*, but without irrigation since their poverty
> will not permit the expense of rebuilding the dam and cleaning
> the ditch. But, because the land is so rich, they have not lost their
> labor.

In 1831 a decree ordered the sale of mission property at public auction; everything was included but the church itself.

On 28 October 1835, during the Texas revolutionary struggle, a volunteer army
headed by Stephen Austin, James Bowie, and James W. Fannin, Jr., sent a ninety-man
advance detachment to find the Mexican position and to select a secure place to camp.
This advance party chose a position near the San Antonio River, a mile from Mission
Concepción, but was attacked by a Mexican cavalry force of some four hundred men.
In the ensuing Battle of Mission Concepción, the Mexicans were repulsed; only one
Texan was lost, but the Mexicans lost sixty men. After the battle, the main Texan army
moved up and used the mission as its campground.

The United States Army took over the mission church for use as a supply depot
during the Mexican War. John R. Bartlett, who visited in 1850, found the church had
been used as a barn or stable. The floor was covered with dung about a foot deep, and
bats flew and chattered above. In 1855 the Bishop of San Antonio turned over what
remained of Mission Concepción to the Brothers of Mary, who had established St.
Mary's School (later St. Mary's University). The Brothers bought adjoining acreage and
used it as a farm to supply the school in town, and as a summer retreat for students
and teachers. They cleaned and restored the church, and in 1861 opened it again for
church services.

Concepción thus avoided the shameful decay of San José. William A. Corner's
1890 book about San Antonio recommends a visit to the building. To do that, however,
the visitor had to fetch the caretaker.

> At the Mission lives a family, which is in charge and some one of
> them will bring you a key to the chapel and show you what
> there is to be seen, but it would be useless to try and elicit any
> information. To them the past of the Mission is as a sealed book
> and it has not romance for them.

Today, only the church building and part of the convento remain, but what there is at
the site is almost entirely original.

MISSION SAN JUAN. By 1794, when the property was partitioned, Mission San Juan had dwindled to almost nothing. Only 36 Indians remained, and of the large mission herds of the past, what survived was meager: a mule, a mare, 2 horses, 4 yokes of oxen, and 55 head of cattle. The population had changed to such an extent by 1815 that of 65 inhabitants, 50 were "Spaniards" and only 15 were Indians. The Indians were destitute, since they   not make a living on what they had. The church was still in good condition, though, and the missionary stationed at Mission Espada took care of the people there, as well. Upon final secularization in 1824, the church and its furnishings were turned over to the priest at the parish church of San Fernando and Mission San Juan ceased to function. The property of the mission was sold at auction, with the exception of the chapel itself.

"Marriage at Mission San Juan" by Theodore Gentilz.

By 1890 the chapel roof had fallen in. Still, it was easier to discern the extent of the mission's layout here and at Espada than at the two larger missions. The chapel walls showed traces of very colorful designs and figures. Of the people living there, Corner remarked:

> A number of Mexican families live here, some of the members of which possess marked Indian features. In the neighborhood of San Juan there are more traces of the Indian in faces and characteristics than anywhere else in Texas.

Beginning in 1907 the church began paying more attention to Mission San Juan: a new roof was built and repairs undertaken. But not until the 1960s was a full program of restoration begun. This included archeological work in the mission compound and the surrounding area.

MISSION ESPADA. Mission Espada was the most isolated and exposed of the missions along the San Antonio River. During its most successful years, perhaps the mission's most significant achievement was a brief book written by one of its priests, Fr. Bartolomé García, in what he said was the most common language among mission Indians. The book, published in Mexico in 1760 and entitled *Manual para administrar los sacramentos*, was used by missionaries to administer the sacraments to Indians.

At the time of partial secularization in 1794, Mission Espada's condition was not much better than that of Mission San Juan. Population was down to only 45, and, of the former mission herds, there was only a cow with a calf, a mare, 3 horses, 3 mules, 8 yokes of oxen, and 1,150 sheep. The latter were not distributed, but rather put in the hands of a shepherd who was supposed to be paid by the community for his services.

The composition of the community also changed rapidly. By 1804, of 94 inhabitants, 37 were Indians and 57 were "Spaniards." Although Espada was supposedly the residence of a missionary serving both Espada and Mission San Juan, this arrangement also appears to have collapsed. By 1813 there was only one missionary, residing at Mission San José, who attended to all four missions.

With final secularization in 1824 came complete neglect. In 1836, during the War for Texas Independence, Bowie and Fannin took over the complex with about one hundred Americans. About two hundred Mexican soldiers tried to dislodge them, but the Americans took defensive positions in the mission and beat back the attack.

By mid-century the Mission Espada church was in ruins. The mission was rescued from total oblivion by a French-born priest, Fr. Francis Bouchu, who came to San Antonio to serve at the Church of San Fernando and developed a special love for Espada. In 1858 he found only the facade and rear wall of the church standing, but he began rebuilding, doing much of the work himself. Eventually, the church was completely restored, and new parish records exist which start with the year 1873. Fr. Bouchu continued his work at Espada until his death in 1907. Corner, who met the priest, said in his 1890 book on San Antonio that Fr. Bouchu was "priest, lawyer, bricklayer, stone mason, photographer, historian, printer."

In 1909 the church at Mission Espada was temporarily closed and services were moved to Mission San Juan. A new restoration was undertaken in 1911, during which a wooden roof replaced the tin one that Fr. Bouchu had built. The church was rededicated in 1915. Additional restoration work was done in the 1930s, '50s, and '60s.

Mission Espada before restoration, ca. 1910.

P

RESERVATION FOR POSTERITY. Initial contacts between the Archdiocese of San Antonio, the recognized owner of the San Antonio missions and their remaining property, and the Federal Government took place in the 1930s. The WPA stabilization, restoration, and reconstruction projects of those years were funded by the government. The church subsequently proposed that the National Park Service take over the missions, but the sites were in such disrepair that Washington deemed the expected restoration and preservation costs prohibitive, and declined.

WPA workmen reconstruct the granary at Mission San José.

The archdiocese then committed $750,000 to the restoration of the mission churches. The work was supervised by O'Neill Ford, a historical architect. The church and the State of Texas also reached an agreement that led to Mission San José becoming a state historic site, and the mission was declared a not-federally-owned national historic site.

The Texas State Parks and Wildlife Department assumed responsibility for administration of the mission, with the cooperation of the Archdiocese and the National Park Service, and the assistance of an advisory board of representatives from all three entities plus the San Antonio Conservation Society and the County of Bexar. Under the arrangement, the Park Service conducted research, including archeology and history, and assisted in restoration, landscaping, repair, and in the elimination of modern accretions. This agreement served as a model for the cooperative agreement eventually reached by the Park Service and the Archdiocese to create a national historical park.

In the 1960s efforts focused on developing a San Antonio Missions Parkway linking the missions and their related sites, and making them more accessible to visitors. Matching federal and local funds were appropriated for this project in the early 1970s. In 1975 the City of San Antonio issued a proposal for an "Old Spanish Missions National Historical Park," and the Park Service responded with a "suitability/feasibility study" detailing alternatives.

After that, things moved apace. House of Representatives Bill No. 14064, "To authorize the establishment of the San Antonio Missions National Historical Park in the State of Texas" was introduced in 1976 by Congressman Abraham Kazen, and sponsored by Senator Lloyd Bentsen. On 27 May the bill was referred to the Committee on Interior and Insular Affairs, and on 10 November 1978 it was signed into Public Law 95-629 by President Jimmy Carter. In San Antonio, Archbishop Patrick Flores and officials from the Department of the Interior and the Texas state govern-

Interior of the church, Mission San José.

ment also signed the document.

The creation of the San Antonio Missions National Historical Park provided a clear legal framework for the preservation of the San Antonio missions and a means to systematize their interpretation for the visiting public. A multitude of institutions, organizations, and interested individuals worked together for years to help preserve, protect, and publicize this unique national historical treasure. Included among them

were the Archdiocese of San Antonio, the San Antonio Conservation Society, the city's government and Chamber of Commerce, and the National Park Service.

The park circumvents for good cause the traditional separation of church and state in the United States. The Park Service leases at no cost the "secular" portions of the mission properties for maintenance and interpretation purposes, while the church maintains control over the "non-secular" portions of the missions.

Church interior, Mission San Juan.

This arrangement is most apparent when a visitor takes a ranger-guided tour of the missions. The ranger escorts visitors to the door of the church, refers to the building in the context of an interpretive talk, and invites them to view the interior if there is no religious function taking place at the time. The ranger then meets the visitors at the other end of the building and continues the tour, without entering the church.

Thus, the Archdiocese preserves control of the mission churches and of whatever historic structures are still used for church purposes, while the Park Service takes care of the rest. Monsignor Balthasar Janacek, liaison officer between the Archdiocese and the Park Service, tells a charming story that illustrates what he calls "the spirit of constant, daily cooperation" that exists between the two institutions. The official ribbon-cutting ceremonies marking the opening of San Antonio Missions National Historical Park took place on Good Friday, I April 1983, at each mission in turn. About 3 P.M., at Mission San Juan, a severe storm blew off part of the roof of a small building, which was to be used by the Park Service but still contained parish property. No maintenance people could be found, so Father Brennan Schmieg, the parish priest, and José Cisneros, superintendent of the newly-opened park, found themselves up on the roof together, nailing down sheets of tin to protect their common interests.

Special legislation passed in November 1990 increased the area of the park by forty percent. The park now includes what remains of all four mission compounds, the Espada dam and the historic San Juan dam, parts of the acequias of all four missions, and the Espada aqueduct. The four missions, the Espada dam and aqueduct, and the San Juan Acequia are listed in the National Register of Historic Sites and Places; Missions San José and Concepción and the Espada dam, acequia, and aqueduct are National Historic Landmarks.

The Espada Aqueduct over Piedras Creek, completed by 1740, still functions.

The dam at Espada still functions, surrounded today by Espada Park on one side of the river and Acequia Park on the other. It brings water from the San Antonio River into the acequia, which today is reduced to a segment several miles long located entirely within park boundaries. Sections of the acequias for the other three missions are now part of the park and, as further studies are conducted, additional remnants may possibly be located and preserved, as well. The Espada aqueduct, which carries

Interior of the church, Mission Espada.

the acequia over Piedras Creek, is a double-arched stone structure that continues to serve its original purpose, even after two centuries of use. It is the only Spanish-built aqueduct still in operation in the United States.

The park also controls some of the old labores at Espada and San Juan. Some of them are still being used for small agriculture, although this form of farming has become increasingly unprofitable. The labores and acequia at San Juan have been incorporated into a Mission San Juan Spanish Colonial Demonstration Farm. The new park boundaries also include the remains of Rancho de las Cabras, Mission Espada's former ranch, located about twenty-five miles south of San Antonio, near the town of Floresville.

Although each of the missions has its individual character, they all had the same general historical background. For purposes of interpretation, the park administration focuses first on common themes of mission history: their shared chronology and development, their place in colonial architecture and art history, their archeology, the similar structure of the mission complexes with their labores and ranches, and their shared culture and tradition. Each mission is then used to interpret different aspects of the story of the Franciscan missions in Texas.

At Mission Concepción the focus is on the mission as a religious center: the history of the Franciscan order and its missionary efforts, conversion of the natives and their religious instruction, and the mission's calendar with its holidays. Here the Park Service also interprets the relationships between church and state in colonial times and between the mission and the surrounding Spanish colonial community.

Church interior, Mission Concepción.

With its reconstructed exterior walls and Indian quarters, Mission San José is used to focus on the protective/defensive character of the mission complex and its perimeter walls, the relation between the missions and nearby presidios, and the danger represented by Apaches and Comanches. At San José rangers also talk about the culture and way of life of the natives, explain the mission's role as a social center to help acculturate Indians to Spanish ways, and describe the daily rhythm of mission life.

Mission San Juan, with its nearby labores, illustrates the mission as an economic center, irrigating the land and producing crops and livestock for its own consumption and for trade with other missions, the nearby presidio and town, and along routes both east to Louisiana and south to Coahuila and other parts of Mexico. At Mission Espada, the focus is on the mission as a vocational education center, teaching essential trades and crafts in the Spanish colonial frontier setting.

POSTSCRIPT: LIVING CONGREGATIONS. The mission churches today are homes to living congregations. Many parishioners today could possibly be descendants of the mission Indians who once lived and labored in these compounds.

Mission San José serves a congregation of 800 families. Mission Concepción is still a "mission:" an outlying or subordinate congregation of St. Cecilia's, a local parish. Concepción also functions as a "chapel of ease" for the people of the surrounding area; that is, a more conveniently accessible church they can attend instead of their home congregation. Mission Espada has 545 families. San Juan, together with its own mission, a subordinate congregation called St. Ann, serves 265 families.

Visitors can still attend Mass at the mission churches. Mass schedules are available at each parish office by phone and are generally posted at the churches. The Sunday noon "mariachi Mass" at Mission San José is a favorite with visitors and local parishioners. Visitors should arrive early, because the church fills up quickly.

Church activities are likely to be going on almost any time at the San Antonio missions, but the *fiestas patronales*, or patron saint's feast days, are full of special events. They are celebrated on or about 3 May at Mission San José, and on or about 26 May at Mission San Juan. At Mission Espada, the fiestas patronales were celebrated traditionally on or around 4 October, the feast of St. Francis. October rains frequently dampened the annual celebration, however, so it is now held in the first week in September.

And no season is more special than Christmas at San José, when the San Antonio Conservation Society and the National Park Service present *Los Pastores*, an old Christmas folk play, usually between New Year's Day and Epiphany, the Feast of the Three Kings (6 January). Performances of Los Pastores have been documented in San Antonio at least as far back as the 1890s.

Mission San José.

ACKNOWLEDGMENTS

My thanks to Adán Benavides and Dora Guerra in San Antonio, Elizabeth John in Austin, and Art Gómez in Santa Fe, all of whom rendered invaluable assistance in this project. My gratitude also to Monsignor Balthasar Janacek, Director for the Old Spanish Missions at the Archdiocese of San Antonio, and to the staff at the San Antonio Missions National Historical Park for their cooperation.

At San Antonio Missions National Historical Park, I wish to single out Superintendent Bob Amdor, Chief of Interpretation Alan Cox, Park Historian Rosalind Rock, and Park Rangers Dan Steed, Gene Warren, Cindy Worthington, John McManness, and Lee Wilder.

Thanks also to Don Schecter and Bill McKinzey for their support and encouragement.

FURTHER READING

Almaráz, Félix D., Jr., *The San Antonio Missions and Their System of Land Tenure*, Austin, Tex.: University of Texas Press, 1989.

Bannon, John Francis, *The Spanish Borderlands Frontier 1513–1821*, Albuquerque, N. Mex.: University of New Mexico Press, 3rd printing, 1979.

Habig, Marion A., *The Alamo Chain of Missions: A History of San Antonio's Five Old Missions*, Chicago, Ill.: Franciscan Herald Press, 1976.

Moorhead, Max L., *The Presidio: Bastion of the Spanish Borderlands*, Norman, Okla.: University of Oklahoma Press, 1975.

Myres, Sandra L., *The Ranch in Spanish Texas, 1691–1800*, El Paso, Tex.: Texas Western Press, 1969.

Newcomb, W. W., Jr., *The Indians of Texas: From Prehistoric to Modern Times*, Austin, Tex.: University of Texas Press, 1961.

Poyo, Gerald E. and Gilberto M. Hinojosa, eds., *Tejano Origins in Eighteenth Century San Antonio*, Austin, Tex.: University of Texas Press, 1991.

San Antonio in the Eighteenth Century, San Antonio, Tex.: Bicentennial Heritage Committee, 1976.

Weber, David J., *The Mexican Frontier 1821–1846: The American Southwest Under Mexico*, Albuquerque, N. Mex.: University of New Mexico Press, 1982.

Cruciform Spanish stirrup, ca. 1600s.

Copyright 1993 by Southwest Parks and Monuments Association, Tucson, Arizona 85701

Library of Congress Number 92-62158

Photography © George H. H. Huey
Edited by Ron Foreman
Book design by Christina Watkins
Typography by TypeWorks, Tucson, Arizona
Lithography by C&C Offset Printing, Co., Inc.
Printed in Hong Kong

Artifacts:

Enrique E. Guerra Collection: pages 7, 18, 22, 28, 31 (thimbles), 34, and 48.
National Park Service: pages 15 and 31 (cloth).
University of Texas at San Antonio: page 11.

Historic Illustrations:

Amon Carter Museum, Fort Worth, Texas: page 38.

Daughters of the Republic of Texas Library, Alamo Plaza, San Antonio, Texas: pages 24, 25, and 42.
Harry Ransom Humanities Research Center Art Collection, University of Texas, Austin, Texas: page 8.
Historic American Buildings Survey, Library of Congress, Washington, D.C.: pages 1, 16–17, 21, 22, 41, and 42–43.
Texas Memorial Museum, Austin, Texas: page 10.
University of Texas, Institute of Texan Cultures, San Antonio, Texas: pages 4–8, 12–16, 19, 27, 30, 33, 40, and 43.
University of Texas, Institute of Texan Cultures, *The San Antonio Light* Collection: page 39.
University of Texas, Institute of Texan Cultures, Courtesy the *San Antonio Express-News*: page 44.